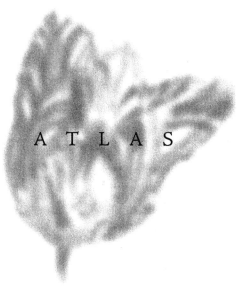

ATLAS

ATLAS

POEMS

Katrine Vandenberg

KATRINA VANDENBERG

For Zed, with best wishes—

Katrine
9/5/12
Winona MN

MILKWEED ○ EDITIONS

Published 2004 by Milkweed Editions
Printed in Canada
Cover and interior design by Christian Fünfhausen
Cover drawings by Jacob Issacz van Swandenburg (1571–1638) and
Adriean Jansz. van Witvelt (c. 1581–1638) are from a book compiled
for auctioning tulip bulbs in early seventeenth-century Holland. Images
used with permission from the National Economic History Archive/
Economic History Library, Amsterdam.
Author photo by Gene Pittman
The text of this book is set in Adobe Jenson.
04 05 06 07 08   5 4 3 2 1
First Edition

Song lyrics on p. 78 from "Tangled Up in Blue" by Bob Dylan.
Copyright © 1974 by Ram's Horn Music. All rights reserved.
International copyright secured. Reprinted by permission.

Milkweed Editions, a nonprofit publisher, gratefully acknowledges
support from Emilie and Henry Buchwald; Bush Foundation; Cargill
Value Investment; Timothy and Tara Clark Family Charitable Fund;
DeL Corazón Family Fund; Dougherty Family Foundation; Ecolab
Foundation; Joe B. Foster Family Foundation; General Mills Foundation;
Jerome Foundation; Kathleen Jones; Constance B. Kunin; D. K. Light;
Chris and Ann Malecek; McKnight Foundation; a grant from the
Minnesota State Arts Board, through an appropriation by the Minnesota
State Legislature, a grant from the National Endowment for the Arts,
and private funders; Sheila C. Morgan; Laura Jane Musser Fund; an
award from the National Endowment for the Arts, which believes that
a great nation deserves great art; Navarre Corporation; Kate and Stuart
Nielsen; Outagamie Charitable Foundation; Qwest Foundation; Debbie
Reynolds; St. Paul Companies, Inc., Foundation; Ellen and Sheldon
Sturgis; Surdna Foundation; Target, Marshall Field's, and Mervyn's
with support from the Target Foundation; Gertrude Sexton Thompson
Charitable Trust (George R.A. Johnson, Trustee); James R. Thorpe
Foundation; Toro Foundation; Weyerhaeuser Family Foundation; and
Xcel Energy Foundation.

Library of Congress Cataloging-in-Publication Data

Vandenberg, Katrina, 1971–
    Atlas : poems / Katrina Vandenberg.—1st ed.
       p. cm.
    ISBN 1-57131-419-9 (pbk. : alk. paper)
 1. HIV-positive men—Poetry. 2. Hemophiliacs—Poetry. 3.
Netherlands—Poetry. I. Title.
    PS3622.A588A95 2004
    811'.6—dc22

                2004006370

This book is printed on acid-free paper.

NATIONAL
ENDOWMENT
FOR THE ARTS

MINNESOTA
STATE ARTS BOARD

FOR MY PARENTS

AND FOR JOHN

A T L A S

ACKNOWLEDGMENTS

I would like to thank the editors of the magazines in which some of these poems first appeared, sometimes in different forms:

Alaska Quarterly Review	"All Those Women on Fine September Afternoons"
American Scholar	"First Lesson: The Anatomist Explains the Primacy of Imagination"
Black Dirt (formerly *Farmer's Market*)	"The Herbalist's Nightshade Song"
Cream City Review	"Essence, Origin"
Florida Review	"Rosary"
Great River Review	"Hunger Winter"
Greensboro Review	"Record"
The Iowa Review	"Remembering Him Dying" "Entertaining Your Father in the Netherlands"
Kerf	"The Third Wonder of the World" "Aphrodisia Song"
Laurel Review	"Jack O'Lantern"

Louisiana Literature	"Red Shoes"
	"The Young Widow's Conception of Faith"
	"Consuming Desire"
	"Nineteen"
	"A Photograph of Marie Florence"
	"The Sunflowers of Arles"
Mid-American Review	"The Problem with the Pills"
New Orleans Review	"Pesto in August"
Poetry Northwest	"Anatomy Lesson #2: The Palpation of Bony Landmarks"
	"The Green Rivers Over Their Faces"
Puerto del Sol	"The Love of Blood"

"The Problem with the Pills" won an AWP Intro Journals Award. "Jack O'Lantern" and "All Those Women on Fine September Afternoons" were reprinted in the Syracuse Cultural Workers' 2002 and 2003 editions of *Women Artists Datebook*.

I would like to thank the J. William Fulbright Scholarship Board, the Netherlands-America Commission for Educational Exchange, and Universiteit Utrecht, especially Wiljan van den Akker and Maarten Prak; and Robert Hedin and the Anderson Center for Interdisciplinary Studies in Red Wing, Minnesota, for giving me time and space to write. I would also like to thank H. Emerson Blake and Milkweed Editions; Mary McDunn and the liberal arts department at the Minneapolis College of Art and Design; Dorianne Laux and Christopher Merrill; the MFA program at the University of Arkansas, especially Pattiann Rogers, John DuVal, and the late James Whitehead; my readers John Reimringer, Michael Downs, Beth Ann Fennelly, and other writers and friends, especially Andrea Clements, Michele Sommer, and Carrie Pomeroy. Most of all, I thank the Haas family, the hemophilia community, Sara Boc and Jamie Stamper, and my parents.

ATLAS

I: TRADE ROUTES

WOMAN IN PLAID SHIRT WRITING A POEM

My sister, who cleans houses, and I are tired

of doing work that no one sees. Like the crew
that spent the morning painting Oprah's lips,

highlighting her cheekbones. And those

who tint the lights to mimic the sun
sparkling on her sweater as she appears

to applause. My sister will pause,

if she is watching, her vacuum off, halfway
through polishing a mirror, annoyed and moved

by a show she's seen before: a woman weeps

because they've made her over, a surprise,
and the camera turns her into pearls of light

cast into ten million rooms.

My sister thinks she's made mistakes—a baby
alone at twenty, a college dropout, most

of her pay in cash she stuffs in envelopes

marked "electricity" and "phone." A plan
that doesn't stop the lights from going out.

Let me start over, from another angle:

Attention makes things beautiful. Vermeer,
you were the kind of man who could do honor

to her poised over an apple on her break.

You'd shine it on your paint-spattered sleeve,
adding vermilion, juice. Illuminate these walls,

this pen, the margins of my morning; keep

me at my desk until this work is done.
Paint me a window into that plush home.

I want her put in the best possible light.

ALL THOSE WOMEN ON FINE SEPTEMBER
AFTERNOONS

When she baked a pie, my mother's hands were blackbirds;
they flecked butter at heaps of sugared apples.
Her hands were wings around the piecrust's edge,
and she fluted it until it swooped around
and down. *Never worry your crust,* she said.

*You love crust like a child; roll it
and imagine it pretty and whole.*

My grandmother could weigh flour
with her hands and measure vinegar with her eyes.
She rolled her crust with a rolling pin
cut by her father from a single apple limb.
My mother cut out star cookies from what was left.

I think about my mother and her mother
and every mother before they came along
on the days I roll out piecrust with the rolling pin
my grandmother gave to me: the rolling pin
that was part of a tree, swelling apples

from blossoms, apples to swell and dimple
crust. My God, think of it, all those women
on fine September afternoons like these,
rolling piecrust and not worrying,
seeing things whole.

A PHOTOGRAPH OF MARIA FLORENCE

sat on my desk my first year
of college, although I never knew
my great-grandmother. I was
sentimental then, dreaming
of telling a future husband, back
in my hometown, that I was pregnant.
She's seventeen, sepia-toned,
a brooch at her neck, her head turned
to look at—a caged songbird?
A view of the organ-grinder
in a German street? A rose pin
gathers her curls at her crown.
I think she holds back a grin. If
she already knew of the trip
she would make to America
on a windfall inheritance;
if her father had begun to sand
the felled oak, making her a box
to hide her trinkets in,
I can't say. The legend goes
her ticket home was stolen,
the Great War broke out, no one
could bring her back again.
She became a mother who burned
letters in German, in the stove,
letting the fire lick the old words
clean. The ashes said *liebe*,
bitte, returning and raining

all over the vineyards on the Sarre
while Maria Florence dreamed
in English, in America,
the trinket of her heart
ticking in a box of secrets.
I already knew by then
that I would never go home.

THE FLOATING

NEW ENGLAND MEDICAL CENTER

When he was dying, she stayed with him all night,
but one night, restless, she walked around a corner
and found a dim hall full of children's breathing
rising from small white beds. She had drifted
into the Floating, the children's hospital boat
being rocked to sleep in the harbor again
the way it was a hundred summers ago.
The horizon of her life had vanished—traffic
lights, students with Chinese takeout boxes
stories down. Now bustled dresses drooped
over the backs of chairs; now immigrant mothers
in flimsy shifts bent over the beds and whispered,
tendrils of hair escaping their tidy knots,
their feet unsteady on the pitch of breath.

FIRST LESSON: THE ANATOMIST
EXPLAINS THE PRIMACY OF IMAGINATION

These fontanelles of your skull won't close
for eighteen months; until then the bones remain
separate plates—frontal, parietal, occipital,
temporal, sphenoid—your concave spinal column
cannot hold. But instead of feeling helpless

when you sense the world outside yourself
and how little you can do, have faith in the world
of your head. Inside there, your skull bones work
to grow together, like the tectonic plates of the earth
in reverse, suturing and shaping as you evolve.

Your head, unlike the earth that sculpts mountains
to the sun, deepens dark grooves within
the brain's hemispheres to hold skeins
of butterflies inside, to show you oceans
and peninsulas without your even opening
your eyes. How different it will be there

from here, where pieces pulled apart until Africa
and Asia hoarded the elephants, and the penguins
clung to a single pole; where we harvest
the pods and seeds of the only spices we can grow,
then send them away in ships, with translators.

When your head is whole with fibrous joints
at the end of these eighteen months, think

how proud some cell in you somewhere will be,
of how its chemical impulse made again

a world with one country, a humming garden,
with the first cervical vertebra, the atlas,
strong enough to hold it all upright.

THE THIRD WONDER OF THE WORLD

I am writing to you and to no one else
here at the hanging gardens of Babylon,
where wide-eyed orchids, long-fingered ferns,
and mandarin oranges spill from terrace
after glazed-brick terrace. Here I am at a wonder
of the ancient world, sweaty in my backpack and boots,
visa rubbing my neck in its hidden pouch.

My guidebook says the gardens were erected
by King Nebuchadnezzar for his wife Amytis
in 562 B.C. My mother says
that you should have come with me, that it is not safe
for a woman to be in a crazy country like this one
alone. A stairway spiders between each terrace.
Fountains spray all of it with water and light.

Only tourists now, no virgin and her damsels
on camels, though it doesn't seem too hard to believe
they would be here, with the women's faces veiled
in black, the robed men jostling against my jeans
making what would be barbarian faux pas
if they were anywhere else.

They call to me, *green eyes*, ask me to finger
the weave of cloth, the smoothness of pottery,
to taste lamb and grapes and rice. But here
in these gardens there is only Amytis
fingering shiny fig leaves and orchid petals,
and the husband who built her a tower

brick by brick on the backs of slaves
to hold plants from all over the world, to keep her
from wondering about the meaning of travel
and the rivers that nurse plants to life.

NEW WORDS

When the skyscrapers fell, I learned the word
burqua: draped in mystery, veiled threat.
Then *jihad* with its ready fist of stones;
Herat erected a mosque with onion domes
on a cerebral ridge. Do all new words
come out of suffering? The older ones fall
more lightly from my lips, having unpacked
their meanings long ago, when they moved in
to English. *English:* variant of the name
of the tribe that landed on Britannia's shores
around the time the *Vandals*—whose name evokes
cartoon graffiti now—first shook Rome's gates
demanding land and sacks of peppercorns.
Still the iambic poems trot on, ignorant
of the Norman Conquest and the burning barn
in which a syllabic forefather first raped the accentual line.
The knowledge rests inside my words, but not me,
I write. Thanksgiving is not far away,
and John bakes pumpkin cheesecake
for a potluck. Dutch spice traders taught my tongue
of cloves; Cortez, *vanilla*—from *vagina:*
black seeds scattered in a free-love frenzy
that ended in smallpox and ruin. I don't know
how many of our words of love arrived
on slave ships, foreign and our own—and now
this new handful flung from the sky. I'll save
this small change, these new words. They are no trade
for a friend or father, but will become my own.

MARRIAGE PORTRAIT OF THE ARNOLFINIS

In the mirror behind the merchant groom and bride, I've seen
the two extra figures: the artist and me—or you.
    The bride's high-waisted green dress is medieval,

their faces flat, and yet that mirror is *modern,*
    demanding we look outside the frame. Look
at the way the artist signs his name above it,

    Jan van Eyck was here, the final sentence
of an age of anonymous art for God.
    We witness Bruges in 1434. The mirror's an eye.

How else can we get in, make sense of people
    as foreign to us as Arnolfini? Think of him,
his gestures too broad for lanterned tavern tables,

    the deals he cuts on cloth while littering the floor
with mussel shells. His tongue an eel strangling
    Flemish verbs. Welcome to the city

where Arnolfini is lost most of the time.
    When he walks over bridges to the wharf at night,
the shut-eyed houses look the same, all cut

    from gingerbread. If there's a moon,
a second city rises in the canals—
    Venezia, with its marzipan domes, mosaics,

mirrors. Did Arnolfini feel that he lived nowhere,
          his world a port whose canals and bridges
reflect each other? Rotterdam, Antwerp,

          Marseilles, Genova . . . was trade the only metaphor
he understood; for instance, did he think,
          when he arranged to have his portrait done,

that the Flemish did light better than the Italians,
          in spite of the rain, because their sun's a rare
gold coin? Because of what Low Country workers do.

          Without materials of their own, in a country born
of the sea and will, they import all they need—
          wool, hops, and Baltic logs. Even the stones that become

their churches are hauled in wagons from France.
          In their hands wool is cloth, and hops are beer,
and logs turn into ships with bellies full

          of cloves and cinnamon. So clay is tiles.
And light is art. *What a strange country,*
          Arnolfini may have thought. What people,

I say, centuries away, to turn
          the raw stuff of life into goods that anyone
might own and use. Thank you, van Eyck,

          for your eye, this marriage. I take this mirror
to be my bridge. I take this day in Bruges.
          I will love and honor you all of my days. I do.

REMEMBERING HIM DYING

It was like his teaching her to ride a bicycle
in the driveway that fall, him calling out
I've got you, which meant he planned to let go
any moment. He made her try again,
again; she crashed the yellow Schwinn
into the elm, cried and called him names.

If she could have looked back and kept her balance
the last time he shoved her out of his hands,
she would have seen him griefstruck, still, shrinking
as she wobbled from his shadow, into the sun-dappled road.

ENTERTAINING YOUR FATHER IN
THE NETHERLANDS

The lies we tell pile up. Your father says
he is happy, and I let him. A friend

of my mother's implores me to admit
that getting involved with you was a mistake

and I say fiercely I would do it again.
Six years after you died I sit with him

on a bench by a canal in Utrecht, eating
Italian *broodjes*, with little to say. We watch

a barge clean the canal for spring, dragging
its claws across the bottom for bicycles tossed

from the bridge by drunken thieves. Pinching
frame after rusted frame, adding each

to the tangle of wheels and handlebars on deck.
I tell him that in Amsterdam two cars

go in each year, and that a Viking ship
was found, intact, at the bottom of the Vecht

after it sank one thousand years ago,
on its way to trade on this very canal.

The ship's in the museum because it's rare;
the bicycles are junk because they aren't,

though they will be rare too if they remain
unfound long enough. Some students pump

their bikes past us with their strong legs—I'm sure
he thinks of you, his youngest son, dead

by twenty-five. I just knew you for five years,
when we were barely grownups, which is why

I'm out of stories any father wants to hear.
What's left are tales of meanness, mistakes, wild foolish

ways you might have outgrown if you lived.
The tales I start, changing their endings when

his smile falters. If you were here, I'd never tell.
But since you're not—speaking of you as pure

and wise is not like we've forgotten you
as much as worried your best face, wearing

it down like a good-luck piece. Listen,
I'm about to tell one that will shock you

back to life, gloriously imperfect and raw.
I've waited until now to bring it up.

II: THE RED FIELDS OF LISSE
(A LOVE STORY)

TULIPOMANIA

In the 1630s, at the height of the frenzy over the tulip bulbs that had recently entered Europe from the Ottoman Empire, Dutch speculators willingly paid more than a merchant's annual salary for a single bulb.

The Dutch had never seen a flower
    with this intensity: the deep purple
        of Viceroys bewitching as black silk,

the scarlet of Gouda that rustled like lust.
    They had never seen such vivid contrasts:
        the golds that threaded through the petals' tapestry,

the crimson that throbbed through cream like blood
    seeping through clean linen. And if they called
        a tulip like this "broken," *broken* was what

they wanted: they could not know the ones they craved
    were brilliant from infection with a virus,
        but must have seen these bulbs were weak and small

and did not breed. Today the mosaic virus
    is gone, and tulips are no longer dear;
        the blooms that fed this fever have long died out.

But aren't you sorry you will never see
    a tulip that would make you offer all
        you own for the layered, translucent promise

in its brown paper wrapper? Aren't you sorry
        you never saw John Keats in his dressing gown,
                scribbling an ode beneath his flowering plum,

will never know the ten thousand men with hemophilia
        infected with HIV two decades ago,
                and the purpose that briefly lit their brilliant veins?

THE LOVE OF BLOOD

Her brothers' dizzy love affairs with blood
too much for her to understand, she dreams
their skin breaks like bud vases; blood shatters
every fluted vein of glass inside their hands.

Their blood could overflow their hearts, then bead
like rain on their lungs. Maybe blood spreads
like velvet wine on people's tongues at church,
transformed inside them by smoke, the power
of the steeple bell. Blood stains their sheets
of muscles, traces roses on their bones.

When they fold socks inside the house and she
plays kickball in the lot, she kicks
for each weak ankle, kicks for the missing factors
in their blood that made a wrong turn in mutated
recessive dreams, that broke the promise
to hold the droplets, lattice-locked, in place.

She feels something is missing. *Greg and Tim
have hemophilia. It means love of blood.
It means their blood has nothing to hold on to,*
said their parents. *Nothing to hold on to.*
At night her brothers fly: the windshield
on the Plymouth splinters in a million pieces.
Glass stars pierce arteries. Highways of blood.

Sometimes when she can't sleep because they moan,
the love of blood deep in their knees, she spreads

herself wide on the bed and feels
the pull of love, of blood inside her;
she takes pain on her smooth white bones for them.

*Hemophilia, a once-incurable, disabling disease usually passed
from mother to son, was transformed into a manageable chronic
illness in the 1960s by the pooled-plasma product, antihemophilic
factor. But the same factor that kept boys out of wheelchairs and
let them lead active lives became infected with the AIDS virus in
the 1980s; from the beginning, factor had been contaminated with
several varieties of hepatitis. Between 1978 and 1985, over half of
the seventeen thousand-person hemophiliac population, as well as
many of their sexual partners and unborn children, were infected
with HIV; almost 90 percent were infected with hepatitis C. Most
hemophiliacs born before the advent of heat-treated factor have
chronic liver disease or are dead.*

THE PROBLEM WITH THE PILLS

She has a problem with the pills that crowd
the tabletop. She has no room to write,
she says, no surface to express herself,
and he feels guilty that he needs to take
so many—or at least to worry her—
or maybe it just bothers both of them
that at age twenty-five he needs to take
so many; neither one can deal with it.
He's not on drugs. These pills are meant to heal.
They are from doctors; they keep him alive.
They are fired like arrows, Federal Expressed
from Bob's progressive pharmacy in LA.
Bob loves his AIDS patients;
he promotes their taking pills.
Bob sends him sunlike vitamins for free,
torpedo AZT pills too;
big, chalky ddI tablets, crisp, grainy moons.
Herbologists send Chinese salvia
like magic in a jar in earthlike clods.
Acyclovir, capsules of blue sky
for herpes zoster. And Bactrim, the worst one,
for Pneumocystis carinii pneumonia,
ancient protozoa that could fill his lungs
with water. He is twenty-five, she thinks,
too young for AIDS, pneumonia, and pills.
She hates the pills, the way they stand, professors'
bottled answers. She hates the way he looks
when he sits slumped and shadowed over them
at night to fish them out of cups

he puts them in at daybreak to keep track of them.
I take forty-six pills a day, he says,
two each hour I'll ever live.
I guess that's not so bad.

Pills are an issue. Pills are real.
They make her think of AIDS and dying,
his daily swallowing of earth and sky.
Who can think of death in sex or daylight,
after all? It's just that constant ritual.
He takes too many pills, and she worries
about him; she worries about them.
Pills never really do
what you tell them anyway. They're just pills.
She takes more pills to compensate
for his pills, mostly lots of aspirin,
and some blue moon pills for sleep and courage.
Even though she loves him, the pills gained all the power.
She knows these pills are meant to heal—at least
hold back the virus while each pill destroys
his pancreas, his stomach, liver. Pills
aren't healing him or them; she wants to talk
about the problem she has with the pills.
But all the words lodge in her throat
and each excuse dissolves.

THE HERBALIST'S NIGHTSHADE SONG

Come and I will clear your throat of lies.
I can brew an antidote to poison gas,
rub ointment on your skin to ease a vine
of muscles' hold on bone. My harvest
cures an epileptic's fit. Can you call belladonna
devil's weed? I warned you of my nightshade
the day it took one, two, three berries
to make a small boy die. I have my signs.

But I have seen my bella donna wander,
and not only to dilate the pupils of cats
who nap in peppermint nearby. At night
she crowns herself in purple flowers;
she holds green and elusive arms to rain
crows and feeds them her black berry eyes.
She has a way of seeping into skin to change

the landscape of your sight, and she will rattle
hearts until the bodies' arms and legs
are still. Mornings my garden is littered
with rabbits and birds who shiver to sleep.
She says to me, I say to you:
trust atropine, trust my hands
to find the miracle in poison.
I wore gloves until I found vision.
Come take my tinctures for your eyes.

RED SHOES

She had red shoes to dance in, snap the soles
across the floor when she was five, a gift
from her grandparents. They didn't know

what days would come. Red shoes,
as red as lights her gandy dancer
grandfather swung in the Pennsalt yard,

twenty-five years of warnings
that trains were switching tracks
and trains were going, they were going

to yellow storm skies in Dakota,
to the maples of Fayetteville Arkansas,
Norwalk Ohio's farms and fences.

They didn't know what days
would come, when she would want the shoes
again, to dance away the strict approach

of her lover's illness, good-byes to yellow houses
of the heart, the closing in of subway trains
to hospitals they must live near.

Oh she is a small woman and men have told her
they like that, but she will tell you that inside
she is an engine, and if she'd choose

she'd dance and dance and dance
away from him and all of it, away
through forests, red lights on her feet

like lanterns in the hills. *What lovely
dancing shoes!* old men will say.
She will not care. She will be going,
going, unable to stop for love or need.

DIPTYCH: BEAUTY AND THE BEAST

I. TOURS, 1945

Cocteau filmed a fairy tale
in his own country
at the end of the war. Slicked
the face of Josette Day
with gloss, wrapped her hair
in a turban to make her look
like a Vermeer
as she hung the sheets
he had scoured the countryside
to find. Filmed her the same morning
his people at the crossroads
stripped a pretty neighbor girl
who had typed for a Nazi
commandant, then shaved
her head. Filmed wearing
a black veil to hide the boils
erupting on his face. Filmed
as the shaved girl bleated
she offered the man no comfort.
Filmed though the film
of our lives does not run
backwards; until the prince
leaped up at the end, shed
of his beastly spell.

2 . BOSTON, 1994

Greg asks to move in
to the room I now write in
to comfort us both and save us
money. It's been two weeks
since his brother, my love,
has died; I can't say a thing.
I take him to the Brattle Theatre
to see Cocteau in black
and white, where it's too dark
to see his jaundiced eyes.
Still, the smell of sugar's
on his breath, the warning sign
of liver failure. Beauty is
the kind of woman I seem
to be, but not the kind
I am: she vanishes *poof*
from her home when the Beast
says he'll die without her,
and look how easily
she billows down
the castle hall like steam
as the curtains wave
like lost summers behind her.

HUNGER WINTER

HAARLEM, 1944

In the end, the ones who live
do so on a rationed piece
of bread, a potato, and one
sugar beet a day. They thicken
their broth with newspaper, butcher
the cat. An old woman queues
in her patched shoes
all afternoon for seed potatoes
and tulip bulbs broken
from the frozen ground. At home,
she slices them for *hutspot,*
the bulbs like shallots, the crackle
of their papery skins answering
the questions of the stove fire
that burns an empty cupboard.
That night for dinner
the woman swallows the spring,
which tastes like sweetened
chestnuts. Eighteen thousand
of the Dutch will die that winter,
including the woman. The bulbs
and seed potatoes will be
among the last to go: the hope,
the strength to wait for the weather
to turn. This time when the bulbs
enter the familiar belly
of the dark, they will not rise
when the sun calls their names.

They will not nod *yes*
in the red fields of Lisse
where the old woman bicycled
with a boy in April, long ago.

ON THE FATE OF THE TULIP SULTAN

Tom Fahey is dead in Boston tonight, the last

of the guys with hemophilia. Tim, I took down
but kept the list we made one night of our friends

who died. Little icons crayoned by their names,

sienna shoes, a midnight truck, a lemon
puppy, for Matt a cherry guitar. Names

that kept coming until we ran out of room.

Tonight Tom's dead. Three hundred years away,
the sultan the Ottomans exiled but let live

embroiders a memory of his tulips

on a tapestry in bright silks. The white stone
of the first full moon in April, the jugglers

who strolled the garden with crayon-colored balls.

Real gold for the flames of candles on the backs
of the tortoises that plodded through the bowers.

A week-long celebration each spring

for the thousand kinds of tulips that he bred.
He doesn't know that as he stitches them

his tulips are beginning to be forgotten.

And three hundred years away only a catalog
of them survives. Does it matter

that already no one else alive remembers

the day you, Greg, and I walked arm in arm
through Central Square; or the New Year's Eve

on the harbor watching fireworks, when the kids

crouching in the trees flung champagne bottles
that hit the street like green exploding stars?

Milton was wrong. It's not just sin we need to see

in order to know it later on, but joy.
One day, when the sultan was old and carving a ring

from jade, he said, *This green is sun through leaves*

on an afternoon in my garden before it bloomed.
My moves with faith are slow; I'm a tortoise

with a candle on its back. Tim, the list

of what I've loved numbers in the thousands.
Surely I'll recognize a thing worth loving

when I see it for the rest of my life.

III: CATALOG OF WANT

HOME ON THE DUTCH
QUEEN'S BIRTHDAY

*Each year on April 29, the Netherlands
celebrates the queen's birthday with an
all-night free market on the sidewalks
among the festivities.*

All night the men wear orange
wigs in the brick streets
without you. You won't be
among the women in gold
foil crowns, picking through
the jettisoned cargo
along the edges of canals
sloshing like lager in the barges'
wakes. Hand-cranked
coffee mills, T-shirts, egg cups,
Old Masters imitations
in gilded frames, warped
records by the local promising
musician who has begun
building sandwiches at the stand
on the Oude Gracht again,
spread out on blankets
and for sale—unbelievable
junk carted down from attics,
and this spring it isn't you
who barely makes it out
in the streetlights' squint
at two AM, mistaking it all
for treasure this one night.

So who will be the one
to toss a guilder in the cup
of the bride with her sign,
"Help Me Pay for My Wedding"?
Who will pay to see themselves
reflected in a mirror
said to be magic on the night
desire goes cheap
as fried rice balls from
Indonesian trailers? No one
can pick you out
of the crowd cheering on
eight costumed men jigging
around a maypole. Another woman
is being led into the center
of their dance, distracted
by a man dressed as a parrot
who tells her each man's day job—
he works at the Spoorweg
museum, Henrik is the only
virgin—and she will be
surprised when the dance ends
as they rush in to raise her
over their heads. She'll kiss
all eight for luck
under the falling confetti
of the crowd's applause,
and she doesn't need you
to tell her how much
in this world still waits
to be noticed and wanted.

APHRODISIA SONG

Tell me about the man you lost or never had
and I'll give you drops of nightshade juice
to widen the black centers of your eyes;
men who look inside them always find

it's time for bed. If he sleeps against the wall,
I will take you to my garden's edge to show you
deep blue throats of jimsonweed; I'll tell you
how its powder on his tongue will part your lips.

Jimsonweed's a nightshade, like mandrake,
henbane. Or these tomatoes here, aphrodisiac
love apples once distrusted for their succulence
and tender skin pulled taut by seed. Some say

they are the true fruit Eve gave Adam in that garden.
No one knows the answer to that one. No one knows
if weak knees, flushed skin, or false visions
from these potions come from poisoning

or heightened love. Take this vial in memory
of mistletoe, and never mind the feverfew.
Witches smoothed nightshade between their thighs
for love and sex. Some of them died. Some flew.

5, RUE AMYOT

You want to condemn the apartment building now converted to a *maison*
for female students in the land of bread wands and Gauloises, where you
were an exchange student, a girl from the heartland, and knew that in one
of these rooms Jeanne Hébuterne had been nineteen like you, and had
had an apartment after the Great War. She turpentined her paintbrushes
here. Cut her hair to look older, as you did. Had a mirror, an artist lover.
On July nights, alone, she lay in bed sticky, billowing her bed sheet over
her like a parachute, watching it settle on her body. She did not brush his
taste of absinthe from her mouth until morning. She pushed aside gauze
curtains, opened a door-shaped window, and jumped, pregnant, two days
after her lover Modigliani died of consumption and said, *Jeanne and I
have agreed upon eternal joy.*

Yes, it was you who laid a sheet of onionskin paper over their shared
grave at Père Lachaise, skating a pencil to watch their names rise from the
lead. No, it was not you but your roommate Michele who rode off on a
motorcycle, straddling the hips of a mechanic from Orly. You lie poorly.
Say it,

you were faithful. You mooned over Ohio boys who did not write back.
But you did not yet know the part about Jeanne ceasing to paint, or his
dragging her through the Luxembourg gardens by her hair. You leapt
with the rest of them to the cobblestoned *rue* nightly. You rose every
morning from white sheets. The house was infested with the big-hearted,
damned dreams of girls falling in love. You don't condemn it. You were
nineteen. You lived there.

NINETEEN

Carrie and I were hanging our wash on the roof
of the hostel in Riomaggiore—all we had carried
in our packs while remaining half-dressed—when
the Italian couple came up to shower. They shared
a stall, not caring about us and our sodden rainbow
of underwear on the line. From the roof
we could see the Mediterranean bang the cliffs,
and other roof gardens, with cats and coral
geraniums like this one. In the shower that morning,
I had sudsed my hair under the open sky,
the fingers of the sun electric, like God's
on the Sistine Chapel ceiling I'd been herded in
to see the week before. Now the cotton partitions
trembled, and the couple's feet danced
in the spray, her small red-painted toes digging
into the tops of his feet. When she cried out,
Carrie looked at me, and I know we were thinking
the same thing, as the couple caterwauled in the tongue
we wanted to learn, and the inbred cats basked,
and our clothes released the grime of early spring,
and the son of the hostel owner went to scout another train.

VERMEER

Every few weeks my backpack bulged not with art books but a towel
and robe, and I passed the tram stop for the Queen's Library in favor of
the seaside town of Scheveningen, where its thermal baths huffed their
lavender breath. Sweet exhalation, undressing to enter a palace of water,
its treasure rooms of steam and snow. Weekday mornings only a handful
of women were scattered in the pools, stretched across the sauna's cedar
altars. One floor below in the dark, they floated in Dead Sea salt tanks.
Outside the baths they had ordinary lives—writing letters, pouring milk,
reaching behind their necks to fasten strings of pearls—lives on the
edge of shifting fast as clouds. Inside they had no story but time, water,
their bodies. Their skin glowed; bubbles twinkled in their glasses of
effervescent water. They laughed beneath the skylights, old friends telling
truths in a language I half-understood. I'd tell you I became one of them,
but we never spoke. I'd tell you, look for yourself, but the windows are all
one way. Go inside, then, where the view of the sea is panoramic and a
snowy towel hangs for you on a silver hook. After a while the attendants
will know you. They will give you apples to crunch your way home.

HONEY, I THINK YOU CAN

When did it happen—when her sex drive
allegedly peaked? when she married?—that suddenly,
beautiful young men are everywhere,
ones she would have snubbed at their age.
But at thirty-two, she's trying to be adult
as she can muster, looking for cocktail invitations
in the gift shop in St. Anthony Park, when the boy at her feet
she did not see at first, restocking thank-you notes,
shakes the hair from his eyes and says
with a slow smile, *Can I help you*
find anything in this big mess? and she wonders
how to answer truthfully
without sweeping all the invitations off the shelf
and getting kicked out for endangering the breakables.
And why, these days, is he always the same boy,
the same rawhide necklace, same cut of his jeans,
the same kind who learns to flirt
with older women like her at the country club
for bigger tips. He's laughing at her, maybe.
Maybe not. Maybe not always the same boy.
What does she know these days
of their haircuts and shoes or how old they are.
It puts her in mind of being on the European backpack circuit
at nineteen, where one night she put herself in danger
on a bus in Padua, not recognizing the Italian signs
for trouble until it had already escalated.
But nothing bad happened to her, nothing
that didn't make a good story better later on.

PESTO IN AUGUST

How many times does this ritual repeat
itself, preparation that begins with sweetness

unlocked by the parting of leaves? How many
women have unpetaled garlic cloves, dripped oil

cold-pressed from olives down a bowl's curve,
ground the edible seeds of pine with mortar

and pestle until the clay was sweet with resin?
Though the legend speaks of love, in Italy

when a woman let basil's scent seep from
her clay-potted balcony, she was being modest

when she said the smell would tell a certain man
to be ready only for her flowers and her smile.

Tonight I steam pasta until my wallpaper curls
from the walls, slice heavy globes of tomatoes

that separate in sighs of juice and seed,
then toss them with hot spaghetti and the green

my garden has produced with sun, wind, earth,
moon, rain; I remember another legend,

that a sprig of basil given
in love seals love forever.

A clink of plates, of silverware, an overflow
of wine. Say, *Love, I am ready. Come. Take. Eat.*

CONSUMING DESIRE

I'm not making this up. In Cafe Latte's wine bar
one of the lovely coeds at the next table
touched John on the arm as if I wasn't there
and said, *Excuse me, sir, but what*
is that naughty little dessert?
And I knew from the way he glanced
at the frothy neckline of her blouse,
then immediately cast his eyes on his plate
before giving a fatherly answer,
he would have given up dessert three months
for the chance to feed this one to her.
I was stunned; John was hopeful;
but the girl was hitting on his cake.
Though she told her friend until they left
she did not want any. I wish she wanted
something—my husband, his cake, both at once.
I wish she left insisting
upon the beauty of his hands, his curls,
the sublimeness of strawberries
and angel food. But she was precocious,
and I fear adulthood is the discipline
of being above desire, cultivated
after years of learning what you want
and where and how, after insisting
that you will one day have it. I don't
ever want to stop noticing a man like the one
at the bar in his loosened tie, reading
the *Star Tribune*. I don't want to eat my cake

with a baby spoon to force small bites,
as women's magazines suggest. And you
don't want to either, do you? You want a big piece
of this world. You would love to have the whole thing.

I MEET MY GRANDMOTHER
IN ITALY

I find her where I least expect her,
Santa Marguerita, with yellow roses
in her hair. She laughs, deep

in the arms of that American GI,
her hair rolled like Hepburn's, her lipstick
red as tiled Verona roofs. Then I remember

the Saturday before she died, the way
we stopped at a greenhouse and she said,
I'll take for my granddaughter all

the plants you have with yellow flowers,
ignoring my protests until the Pontiac
was heaped with roses and verbena,

with lemon gladiola perfume I could gather
in my hands. She said, *Take them*
all; you need to have a happy life.

THE SUNFLOWERS OF ARLES

Before the bullet, before the hover
of crows, was the waking up
in the yellow house to the palette of the south—
the sky lapis lazuli, and the lemon
sheen of believing that it would never rain
again; there was a morning spent
wresting the cables of sunflower stalks
from the field, there was yellow excess
unafraid to migrate into waste.
And after the February lindens,
the sideways rains of Nuenen, after
the failure at serving God, was the need

to make the artist coming to live with him
the present of a beautiful room,
to arrange sunflowers in a vase
and mix a palette of gold coins,
sulphur, buttercream, olive oil,
and smog, his father's biblical pages,
the unkempt hair of that sad
café dancer, to slash his brush
through jags of paint each day

until a dozen canvases were strewn
drying, their gold pools rancid butter
in the heat, ready to festoon
the walls. There was a rearrangement
of the guest room, the smoothing

of its quilt, consideration of his own
yellow-streaked beard in the mirror,
and the eyes coming to replace
his looking in—here—to this silver spot.

There was. And though I am a soothsayer
who cheats, a prophet of the past
who knows about the yellow
houses of promise, I do not think
he should have known
how this would end. Before
he painted himself out of the asylum
on inky paths through tortuous
trees, before turning jaundiced
eyes toward sun-flowered days
to say he had been a fool again,

he had a month of mornings
just like that one,
and evenings when he walked
the dusty street after work; exhausted,
to douse bread in bouillabaisse
and chat up the captive barmaid, glad
for canvases newly framed and nailed
in place upstairs, for the perfume
of lead paint and anticipation
stinging the empty room.

IV: THE ART OF FINDING

FIRST SNOWFALL IN ST. PAUL

This morning in the untouched lots
    of Target, St. Agnes, and Lake
        Phalen, girls all over the city
            in the first snowfall
        of their sixteenth year are being asked
    by brothers, fathers—my cousin
Warren—to drive too fast then lock
    their brakes, to teach them how to right
        themselves. The whine of the wheels, the jerk
            when they catch—from Sears to Como Park
        to Harding High, the smoke
    that bellows from their lungs,
        the silver sets of jagged
            keys, the spray of snow,
                the driver's seat, the encouraging *Go*

ENGINE

*From Latin: natural disposition or talent, beget,
more at* kin. *Machine converting energy into
mechanical force and motion.*

Spark plugs igniting gasoline. Interchangeable
parts installed in Romulus on the line.
Jim's two UAW boys scrub grease
from their hands at the end of their shift.
Powerful spider legs fan across their palms
like the highways on the map that shatter
from Detroit to the plants: the Rouge,
Dearborn, Gibraltar, Highland Park.
The roads they drive to drink beer in Wyandotte.

They meet their father Jim there, at Louie's Bar
across from the Pennsalt rail yard
where he's foreman. Hunch at the counter
cracking peanuts over sweating bottles
from the plant on Gratiot Road. A nod
to the barmaid. Shake hands
with the switchman, the gandy dancer. Outside
the trains clack and grind
like the steam freights that first rolled west
on the Great Northern line, on track

Jim's father laid. At a job interview
he proved he had experience by holding out
his hands to show his missing fingers.
One afternoon his ribs plinked
like a xylophone, broken one

by one when he was caught between
two cars. Whiskey buffed his heart
to a white-hot shine. The whistle, the lantern,
the signal, the distance. He abandoned
his wife and child on a homestead
near the Red River, got a second chance
when she turned up as a cook in a camp
in Oregon. He was maimed,
he said. No one could write to her.
No one questions the truth of this.

The track, the open road, gear teeth, fuel,
exhaust, ignition. Two boys in Detroit
understand force and action,
reaction. They drive a Chevrolet west
to the Dakotas, Montana, and on to the sea,
pleased at living in an empire
on its upswing, believing that because
they built some thing, that marking
the way between here and there
makes it belong to them.

ROSARY

Today I strip each Gallica and Damask bush;
today I fill each pillowcase I have
with crimson petals. My roses cannot last
the three-month wagon ride to Texas.
I've spent these last two weeks in Charleston
pounding my roses to paste.

Simmer and cool and simmer again, and rose
paste blackens to clay. I gloss my hands
with rose oil then and roll the clay to beads.
With a needle I pierce each one and string them
on wire to dry—one group in five, the rest in tens
for Glory Bes, the Act of Faith, the Mysteries.

On the trails that wind to Oregon and Texas
like a vine's memory of a trellis, some women
water anxiously, packing soil and blankets
around their roses' roots, and still they drip
trails of petals; bushes planted to the side
mean children lie dead underneath. On my way

in June I'll say my decades every night:
summers spent with fish heads brought in
from the Stono River, wax poured on branches
I scarred with scissors. I'll count and recount
the Joyful Mysteries, the children who bloomed
in wombs where none had been before.

But what will petal the eyes of our dead? What
will braid the hair of our brides? Blessed Mother,
let these beads do as any rosary should:
let me concentrate on the Mysteries instead
of counting the times I've said the prayers.
Let my beads keep me from losing my place.

ESSENCE, ORIGIN

I like to think of it like this: a woman drenches
rinds with olive oil in a ceramic crock and leaves
them overnight. She comes the next day to strain
and the mixture is Christmastime in Alabama,

satsumas in a sack and kites and almonds.
She presses with her fingers to release more
orange oil, and then it's China oranges in baskets,
two for a penny in St. Michael's square, crescent moon

peels awash in the Thames. She adds
the delicate skins of lemon-shaped Jaffas
and on the second day the oil froths into orange
flowers, thick as lace, snow on windows in Brazil.

The third day is bitters, as Seville oranges
are squeezed into syrup, then nothing
the next day but the white skin that bursts
from orange centers like spiderwebs and asters.

The oil continues to attract oil, to distill as
she adds the peels of navels on the fifth day
and thinks about the start of a whole
new orange, tight as a secret in the apex.

On the sixth day the elixir becomes the oranges
first spilled by Moors on the market tables of Florence
and traded for leather. And the base of the essence
on its last day reminds her of nothing so much

as wonder for the tree in northern India that first
offered one wild sun back to the sky, conjured forth
from white blooms dense as a tree's dream for light,
rain from the Ganges, Himalayan soil, strong roots.

THE YOUNG WIDOW'S
CONCEPTION OF FAITH

After he died, a stranger planted a tree for him,
an olive in the rock of Israel. When his widow
washed her dish and swept her porch, she thought
about him growing there, sap turned to blood.
Years later when she has grown still more
and been married again and blessed more times
than she can count, the tree will curl its leaves
upon the bluest sky and shed branches in peace.
Oil will be pressed and flow from his fruit, softening
a woman's skin, a crust of bread, lighting
a rag lamp after dark. His branches will be spoons,
whistles, umbrellas, and strangers everywhere
will smell his unbruised olive flesh and hold him,
loving the straightness of his olive bones.

ANATOMY LESSON #2: THE PALPATION
OF BONY LANDMARKS

To color them in on a skeleton chart
is nothing like pinpointing them on your body,
so we sit face to face in the art of finding;
zygoma is nothing but the curve of your cheek,
and next are both your clavicles, collaring
your neck. They meet at a hook, the sternal notch

at the edge of all that's fragile—a little box
that holds your voice, your throat delivering
each breath. Too much to think about just now;
I'd rather think of how your bones protect.
The plate of your breast is smooth and firm,
a locked door to the ribbed cage keeping safe
your heart forever. This is true to a point,

the point where bones end:
if I follow your sternum down
to the xiphoid process, I touch the place
where nearly nothing holds your liver or spleen.
But here we are, in the place where bones
meet skin, and what a miracle you are,
a landscape I have lived with and never seen
until now. What a difficult gift,
to touch and know the architecture
holding you upright beneath your surface.

THE GREEN RIVERS OVER THEIR FACES

Whatever other people say, the two sisters know
their mother is alive. Tess says she combs
the fog with rubied hands, helping the ghost
freighters part the Great Lakes. Irene is sure
that on a deserted island she's snapping fires
to life from wet sand and seaweed, signaling
the planes that she must fly, her girls are waiting
and awake on the lighted coastline. They have

her shoes. A strange man found them on the end
of the dock, neat and jeweled and left to right.
Their father took the slippers, said no
when the police said suicide.
Tess gave Irene the left one;
they've slept with them all winter. As a pair,
they make them tramp and echo on the stairs.

In April, when a neighbor finds her body
blue and current-trapped beneath a boathouse,
where she slept so long among the cattails
the coldest police dog nose could not wake her,
the sisters neatly shelve her shoes away,
left to right in her closet, the way she likes.
And still they wait. Because some nights she rises
barefoot from November's water and their basement,
her hair streaming green rivers
over their faces until they wake.

TONIGHT I CAN WRITE THE SADDEST LINES

AFTER NERUDA

Tonight I can write the saddest lines.
Write for instance, *The world cares nothing for us.*
It tosses night over us like a cloth on the cage of a squawking bird
and the tulips have closed in shame.
Tonight I can write the saddest lines.
He and I loved each other and thought the world loved us too.

To think he has slipped from my hands like a fish, to his death.
To think I thought I could weave love and words into a net.
Look. The Great Lakes are even bigger and deeper without him.
And my poems wash through the sieve of my heart.

A lovely voice not far away is singing. I have no pleasure
in the obscene mouths of the tulips because I have lost him.
The world cares about no one. I have closed in shame.

We no longer need the dead, that's for sure,
but how we needed them. How we squawked that the wind
should love the cochleas of their ears because we did;
how much it mattered to us that our voices
made the waters of those caves quiver. The dead belong
to the lakes and the ground. As do my history, my cells.
Their tongues and the word *always.*

Our lives are so short and the Great Lakes will live so long,
manufacturing outlandish fish,

stringing chains of eels and bacteria to eat each other.
We know that we no longer need the dead, but maybe we do need them.
How we repeat the words they left behind.
How hungry we are for their stories.

FINDING A BOOK I FORGOT HE OWNED
AT THE USED BOOKSTORE YEARS
AFTER HIS DEATH

But I have more books at home than I can read,
and much of what I've read I can't remember.
Everyone I know shares this predicament.

It is hard to get people to care about stories
of the dead. They yellow, pile in dusty stacks.

SUPPOSE

And what if you could step outside yourself,
could walk the streets of your old life after dark
until you found yourself in the lit window
of the bungalow on the April night you packed
your dead lover's clothes in a box you weighted
with his shoes, and saw yourself opening your arms

to fold his shirts? And then walked on. What if
we all could be this generous, cleaving ourselves
from the brief gasps of lilacs in our own yards,
from the outgrown rooms with their sticks of incense
dropping their thin threads of ash?
What if we were willing to turn the corner

to walk the street that holds the sum of lives,
the gallery of women taping shut
the boxes of the clothes of the dead, labeling them
with permanent marker? Oh, and if we did not try

to say we knew what was inside
their Glad bags, rustling secrets from the curb,
but spoke of those boxes and bags in such a way
that everyone who listened could open them and find

the shirts and shoes of their own dead brothers,
and discarded hearts, the whispers
of missing sisters across twin beds, old letters,

old dolls, the names for unnamed terrors,
the trinkets they'd forgot—what if you could
make everyone rich with the things they had lost?
Wouldn't you be that generous, if you knew how?

JACK O'LANTERN

My sister and I grew pumpkins, Cinderellas
by the vineful, until they nudged the feet
of Daddy's Sugar Snow corn. She
remembers waiting—waiting for their shells
to quicken with rain and each moon's phase,
waiting for our father to carve the faces
we drew on the pumpkin with pencil, because
he said that girls could cut themselves with knives.

Here is what nobody seems to remember:
she was nineteen and pregnant and apologetic.
I was twelve, and we were both aware that in fall
all things are round: apples and raindrops,
harvest moons, squash. She asked him to carve
the smallest pumpkin in the patch for the baby
and our father walked out, left us alone, two girls,
three pumpkins, slotted spoons, a butcher knife.

In the mirror the dark made of the kitchen window,
blushed by leaves, I asked her not to cry. Instead,
she cut into a pumpkin's head and scraped
its wet insides from grainy walls, and then
abandoned her spoon. Her fingers wrested
seeds from the pale gourd pulp until they slid,
separated from its skull through her hands,
first as droplets, then as strings of pearls.

She said, *We don't need Father anymore.*
We can carve this ourselves. Watch me
slice out lips and eyes where none has been before.
When she hunched to light the votive,
it sputtered, then it glowed. And after, when
we went outside to look at her finished lantern
from the road, I said I liked the way her light
shone through the face that flickered in the dark.

MATURITY

Back then we thought it meant doing
what you wanted
and we were proud of Michele

for dumping the art school in New York
to run off
to Switzerland with a man

she'd met there the summer before.
He was older,
elfin, a man who said he wanted

to buy her a house in the Alps,
but first
had to learn a fifth language,

live six months on the Amazon.
To help pay
for the room they shared, she took a job

we thought glamorous, lying
on her back
on a scaffold, filling holes in a church fresco

pitted by a mob during the Reformation.
She had to mix
her blues a little darker than the ones

used eight centuries before to paint
the Virgin's robes,
so anyone could tell at a glance

what work was hers, and what the artist's.
It was boring,
she said. Michele, I misunderstood

and then misunderstood again, using
the word *maturity*
as a reason not to act, to shy away

from the bold strokes of risk. You
came home, alone,
broke, and broken, for a while, saying

the job was meditative, that you found
things as you lay there.
One day a strand of the artist's wavy hair

in the Virgin's forehead, and another day,
stray strands of horsehair
from his brush embedded in her blue robes.

MARRYING LATE

When I think of what it means not to marry
the high school sweetheart, but to find each other
as we did at ages thirty and forty, I think
of John and I singing along to an old cassette
of Jackson Browne on car trips, and how, as we sing,
a part of me is hearing the song for the first time
in Detroit, on WRIF with my first boyfriend
in his truck as he took curves, shifting hard and fast.
And probably John is making love with a black-haired girl
in the carpeted back of his van in 1979, out west,
the cassette new and popular, draining the battery.
How unlikely that we ended up traveling together
singing a song we each learned with someone else.
Neither of us minds that, the way we might have then.

RECORD

Late night July, Minnesota,
John asleep on the glassed-in porch,
Bob Dylan quiet on a cassette

you made from an album
I got rid of soon after
you died. Years later,

I regret giving up
your two boxes of vinyl,
which I loved. Surely

they were too awkward,
too easily broken
for people who loved music

the way we did. But tonight
I'm in the mood for ghosts,
for sounds we hated: pop,

scratch, hiss, the occasional
skip. The curtains balloon;
I've got a beer; I'm struck

by guilt, watching you
from a place ten years away,
kneeling and cleaning each

with a velvet brush before
and after, tucking them in
their sleeves. Understand,

I was still moving then.
The boxes were heavy.
If I had known

I would stop here
with a husband to help me
carry, and room—too late,

the college kids pick over
your black bones on Mass. Ave.,
we'll meet again some day

on the avenue but still,
I want to hear it,
the needle hitting the end

of a side and playing silence
until the arm gives up,
pulls away.

NOTES

"The Floating." At the turn of the century, the Floating Hospital boat traveled the Boston Harbor giving tenement children the sea air doctors believed would cure them of typhoid, cholera, and whooping cough. The Floating Children's Trauma Unit is now part of New England Medical Center.

"Entertaining Your Father in the Netherlands" is for Paul Haas, who actually shocks less easily than I do.

"Tulipomania" and "On the Fate of the Tulip Sultan." Information on the mosaic virus and Ahmed III, who reigned in the early 1700s and instigated a resurgence of interest in the tulip, came from Mike Dash's *Tulipomania: The Story of the World's Most Coveted Flower and the Extraordinary Passions It Aroused* (New York: Crown Publishers, 1999), 58–61, 196–207.

Information on hemophilia and AIDS in the note at the end of "The Love of Blood" comes from *Blood Saga: Hemophilia, AIDS, and the Survival of a Community* by Susan Resnik (Berkeley: University of California Press, 1999), ix, 1; the National Hemophilia Foundation; and the Centers for Disease Control.

"Diptych: Beauty and the Beast." In 1945, the French government asked Jean Cocteau to make a film to uplift the people. The trials of making *La belle et la bête* are recorded in *Professional Secrets: An Autobiography of Jean Cocteau Drawn from His Lifetime Writings* by Robert Phelps and translated by Richard Howard (New York: Farrar, Straus, and Giroux, 1970.)

"Record." The snippet of the song "Tangled Up in Blue" is from Bob Dylan's album *Blood on the Tracks*.

GENE PITTMAN

KATRINA VANDENBERG was raised in the Downriver area of Detroit, and her poems have appeared in *American Scholar, The Iowa Review, Alaska Quarterly Review, Poetry Northwest,* and other magazines. She was a 1999–2000 Fulbright fellow to the Netherlands and a hemophilia-AIDS activist and is currently the visiting writer at the Minneapolis College of Art and Design. She lives with her husband, fiction writer John Reimringer, in St. Paul.

MORE POETRY FROM MILKWEED EDITIONS

*To order books or for more information, contact Milkweed
at (800) 520-6455 or visit our Web site (www.milkweed.org).*

TURNING OVER THE EARTH
Ralph Black

MORNING EARTH:
Field Notes in Poetry
John Caddy

**THE PHOENIX GONE, THE
TERRACE EMPTY**
Marilyn Chin

**TWIN SONS OF DIFFERENT
MIRRORS**
Jack Driscoll and Bill Meissner

INVISIBLE HORSES
Patricia Goedicke

**THE ART OF WRITING:
LU CHI'S WEN FU**
Translated from the Chinese by
Sam Hamill

PLAYING THE BLACK PIANO
Bill Holm

BUTTERFLY EFFECT
Harry Humes

GOOD HEART
Deborah Keenan

THE LONG EXPERIENCE OF LOVE
Jim Moore

**THE PORCELAIN APES OF MOSES
MENDELSSOHN**
Jean Nordhaus

**SONG OF THE WORLD BECOMING:
NEW AND COLLECTED POEMS
1981-2001**
Pattiann Rogers

MILKWEED EDITIONS

Founded in 1979, Milkweed Editions is the largest independent, nonprofit, literary publisher in the United States. Milkweed publishes with the intention of making a humane impact on society, in the belief that good writing can transform the human heart and spirit. Within this mission, Milkweed publishes in five areas: fiction, nonfiction, poetry, children's literature for middle-grade readers, and the World As Home—books about our relationship with the natural world.

JOIN US

Milkweed depends on the generosity of foundations and individuals like you, as well as on the sales of its books. In an increasingly consolidated and bottom-line driven publishing world, your support allows us to select and publish books on the basis of their literary quality and the depth of their message. Please visit our Web site (www.milkweed.org) or contact us at (800) 520-6455 to learn more about our donor program.

INTERIOR DESIGN BY CHRISTIAN FÜNFHAUSEN.

TYPESET IN 11/15 ADOBE JENSON.

PRINTED ON ACID-FREE 50# FRASER TRADE BOOK PAPER

BY FRIESEN CORPORATION.